Welcome Little One!

_____

_____

Guest Name

_____

Baby Predictions

Date of Birth: _____

Time of Birth: _____

Weight: _____   Height: _____

Hair Color: _____

Eye Color: _____

Resemblance: ☐ Mom   ☐ Dad

I hope the baby gets mom's:

_____

I hope the baby gets dad's:

_____

Advice for the Parents

_____

_____

_____

_____

Well Wishes for the Baby

_____

_____

_____

_____

Guest Name

_____

Baby Predictions

Date of Birth: _____

Time of Birth: _____

Weight: _____   Height: _____

Hair Color: _____

Eye Color: _____

Resemblance: ☐ Mom   ☐ Dad

I hope the baby gets mom's:

_____

I hope the baby gets dad's:

_____

Advice for the Parents

_____
_____
_____
_____
_____

Well Wishes for the Baby

_____
_____
_____
_____
_____

Guest Name

_____

Baby Predictions

Date of Birth: _____
Time of Birth: _____
Weight: _____   Height: _____
Hair Color: _____
Eye Color: _____
Resemblance: ☐ Mom   ☐ Dad

I hope the baby gets mom's:
_____

I hope the baby gets dad's:
_____

Advice for the Parents

_____
_____
_____
_____
_____

Well Wishes for the Baby

_____
_____
_____
_____
_____

Guest Name

_____

Baby Predictions

Date of Birth: _____

Time of Birth: _____

Weight: _____   Height: _____

Hair Color: _____

Eye Color: _____

Resemblance: ☐ Mom   ☐ Dad

I hope the baby gets mom's:

_____

I hope the baby gets dad's:

_____

Advice for the Parents

_____
_____
_____
_____

Well Wishes for the Baby

_____
_____
_____
_____
_____

Guest Name

_____

Baby Predictions

Date of Birth: _____
Time of Birth: _____
Weight: _____   Height: _____
Hair Color: _____
Eye Color: _____
Resemblance: ☐ Mom   ☐ Dad

I hope the baby gets mom's:
_____

I hope the baby gets dad's:
_____

Advice for the Parents

_____
_____
_____
_____
_____

Well Wishes for the Baby

_____
_____
_____
_____
_____

Guest Name

_____

Baby Predictions

Date of Birth: _____
Time of Birth: _____
Weight: _____ Height: _____
Hair Color: _____
Eye Color: _____
Resemblance: ☐ Mom ☐ Dad

I hope the baby gets mom's:
_____

I hope the baby gets dad's:
_____

Advice for the Parents

_____
_____
_____
_____
_____

Well Wishes for the Baby

_____
_____
_____
_____
_____

Guest Name

_____

Baby Predictions

Date of Birth: _____

Time of Birth: _____

Weight: _____   Height: _____

Hair Color: _____

Eye Color: _____

Resemblance: ☐ Mom   ☐ Dad

I hope the baby gets mom's:

_____

I hope the baby gets dad's:

_____

Advice for the Parents

_____

_____

_____

_____

_____

Well Wishes for the Baby

_____

_____

_____

_____

Guest Name

_____

Baby Predictions

Date of Birth: _____
Time of Birth: _____
Weight: _____   Height: _____
Hair Color: _____
Eye Color: _____
Resemblance: ☐ Mom   ☐ Dad

I hope the baby gets mom's:

_____

I hope the baby gets dad's:

_____

Advice for the Parents

_____
_____
_____
_____

Well Wishes for the Baby

_____
_____
_____
_____
_____

Guest Name

_____

Baby Predictions

Date of Birth: _____
Time of Birth: _____
Weight: _____   Height: _____
Hair Color: _____
Eye Color: _____
Resemblance: ☐ Mom   ☐ Dad

I hope the baby gets mom's:
_____

I hope the baby gets dad's:
_____

Advice for the Parents

_____
_____
_____
_____
_____

Well Wishes for the Baby

_____
_____
_____
_____

Guest Name

_____

Baby Predictions

Date of Birth: _____

Time of Birth: _____

Weight: _____ Height: _____

Hair Color: _____

Eye Color: _____

Resemblance: ☐ Mom   ☐ Dad

I hope the baby gets mom's:

_____

I hope the baby gets dad's:

_____

Advice for the Parents

_____
_____
_____
_____
_____

Well Wishes for the Baby

_____
_____
_____
_____
_____

Guest Name

_____

Baby Predictions

Date of Birth: _____

Time of Birth: _____

Weight: _____   Height: _____

Hair Color: _____

Eye Color: _____

Resemblance: ☐ Mom   ☐ Dad

I hope the baby gets mom's:

_____

I hope the baby gets dad's:

_____

Advice for the Parents

_____

_____

_____

_____

Well Wishes for the Baby

_____

_____

_____

_____

_____

Guest Name

_____

Baby Predictions

Date of Birth: _____

Time of Birth: _____

Weight: _____   Height: _____

Hair Color: _____

Eye Color: _____

Resemblance: ☐ Mom   ☐ Dad

I hope the baby gets mom's:
_____

I hope the baby gets dad's:
_____

Advice for the Parents

_____

_____

_____

_____

Well Wishes for the Baby

_____

_____

_____

_____

_____

Guest Name

_____

Baby Predictions

Date of Birth: _____

Time of Birth: _____

Weight: _____   Height: _____

Hair Color: _____

Eye Color: _____

Resemblance: ☐ Mom   ☐ Dad

I hope the baby gets mom's:

_____

I hope the baby gets dad's:

_____

Advice for the Parents

_____

_____

_____

_____

_____

Well Wishes for the Baby

_____

_____

_____

_____

_____

Guest Name

_____

Baby Predictions

Date of Birth: _____
Time of Birth: _____
Weight: _____   Height: _____
Hair Color: _____
Eye Color: _____
Resemblance: ☐ Mom   ☐ Dad

I hope the baby gets mom's:
_____

I hope the baby gets dad's:
_____

Advice for the Parents

_____
_____
_____
_____
_____

Well Wishes for the Baby

_____
_____
_____
_____
_____

Guest Name

_____

Baby Predictions

Date of Birth: _____

Time of Birth: _____

Weight: _____   Height: _____

Hair Color: _____

Eye Color: _____

Resemblance: ☐ Mom   ☐ Dad

I hope the baby gets mom's:

_____

I hope the baby gets dad's:

_____

Advice for the Parents

_____

_____

_____

_____

_____

Well Wishes for the Baby

_____

_____

_____

_____

_____

Guest Name

_____

Baby Predictions

Date of Birth: _____
Time of Birth: _____
Weight: _____   Height: _____
Hair Color: _____
Eye Color: _____
Resemblance: ☐ Mom   ☐ Dad

I hope the baby gets mom's:
_____

I hope the baby gets dad's:
_____

Advice for the Parents

_____
_____
_____
_____
_____

Well Wishes for the Baby

_____
_____
_____
_____
_____

Guest Name

_____

Baby Predictions

Date of Birth: _____

Time of Birth: _____

Weight: _____   Height: _____

Hair Color: _____

Eye Color: _____

Resemblance: ☐ Mom   ☐ Dad

I hope the baby gets mom's:

_____

I hope the baby gets dad's:

_____

Advice for the Parents

_____
_____
_____
_____
_____

Well Wishes for the Baby

_____
_____
_____
_____

Guest Name

_____

Baby Predictions

Date of Birth: _____
Time of Birth: _____
Weight: _____ Height: _____
Hair Color: _____
Eye Color: _____
Resemblance: ☐ Mom ☐ Dad

I hope the baby gets mom's:
_____

I hope the baby gets dad's:
_____

Advice for the Parents

_____
_____
_____
_____
_____

Well Wishes for the Baby

_____
_____
_____
_____

Guest Name

_____

Baby Predictions

Date of Birth: _____

Time of Birth: _____

Weight: _____   Height: _____

Hair Color: _____

Eye Color: _____

Resemblance: ☐ Mom   ☐ Dad

I hope the baby gets mom's:

_____

I hope the baby gets dad's:

_____

Advice for the Parents

_____

_____

_____

_____

_____

Well Wishes for the Baby

_____

_____

_____

_____

_____

Guest Name

_____

Baby Predictions

Date of Birth: _____
Time of Birth: _____
Weight: _____   Height: _____
Hair Color: _____
Eye Color: _____
Resemblance: ☐ Mom   ☐ Dad

I hope the baby gets mom's:
_____

I hope the baby gets dad's:
_____

Advice for the Parents

_____
_____
_____
_____

Well Wishes for the Baby

_____
_____
_____
_____
_____

Guest Name

_____

Baby Predictions

Date of Birth: _____
Time of Birth: _____
Weight: _____   Height: _____
Hair Color: _____
Eye Color: _____
Resemblance: ☐ Mom   ☐ Dad

I hope the baby gets mom's:
_____

I hope the baby gets dad's:
_____

Advice for the Parents

_____
_____
_____
_____

Well Wishes for the Baby

_____
_____
_____
_____
_____

Guest Name

_____

Baby Predictions

Date of Birth: _____

Time of Birth: _____

Weight: _____   Height: _____

Hair Color: _____

Eye Color: _____

Resemblance: ☐ Mom   ☐ Dad

I hope the baby gets mom's:

_____

I hope the baby gets dad's:

_____

Advice for the Parents

_____
_____
_____
_____
_____

Well Wishes for the Baby

_____
_____
_____
_____
_____

Guest Name

_____

Baby Predictions

Date of Birth: _____

Time of Birth: _____

Weight: _____   Height: _____

Hair Color: _____

Eye Color: _____

Resemblance: ☐ Mom   ☐ Dad

I hope the baby gets mom's:

_____

I hope the baby gets dad's:

_____

Advice for the Parents

_____

_____

_____

_____

Well Wishes for the Baby

_____

_____

_____

_____

Guest Name

_____

Baby Predictions

Date of Birth: _____
Time of Birth: _____
Weight: _____   Height: _____
Hair Color: _____
Eye Color: _____
Resemblance: ☐ Mom   ☐ Dad

I hope the baby gets mom's:
_____

I hope the baby gets dad's:
_____

Advice for the Parents

_____
_____
_____
_____
_____

Well Wishes for the Baby

_____
_____
_____
_____
_____

Guest Name

_____

Baby Predictions

Date of Birth: _____

Time of Birth: _____

Weight: _____   Height: _____

Hair Color: _____

Eye Color: _____

Resemblance: ☐ Mom   ☐ Dad

I hope the baby gets mom's:

_____

I hope the baby gets dad's:

_____

Advice for the Parents

_____
_____
_____
_____

Well Wishes for the Baby

_____
_____
_____
_____
_____

Guest Name

_____

Baby Predictions

Date of Birth: _____

Time of Birth: _____

Weight: _____   Height: _____

Hair Color: _____

Eye Color: _____

Resemblance: ☐ Mom   ☐ Dad

I hope the baby gets mom's:

_____

I hope the baby gets dad's:

_____

Advice for the Parents

_____

_____

_____

_____

_____

Well Wishes for the Baby

_____

_____

_____

_____

_____

Guest Name

_____

Baby Predictions

Date of Birth: _____
Time of Birth: _____
Weight: _____   Height: _____
Hair Color: _____
Eye Color: _____
Resemblance: ☐ Mom   ☐ Dad

I hope the baby gets mom's:
_____

I hope the baby gets dad's:
_____

Advice for the Parents

_____
_____
_____
_____
_____

Well Wishes for the Baby

_____
_____
_____
_____

Guest Name

_____

Baby Predictions

Date of Birth: _____

Time of Birth: _____

Weight: _____   Height: _____

Hair Color: _____

Eye Color: _____

Resemblance: ☐ Mom   ☐ Dad

I hope the baby gets mom's:

_____

I hope the baby gets dad's:

_____

Advice for the Parents

_____

_____

_____

_____

_____

Well Wishes for the Baby

_____

_____

_____

_____

_____

Guest Name

_____

Baby Predictions

Date of Birth: _____

Time of Birth: _____

Weight: _____   Height: _____

Hair Color: _____

Eye Color: _____

Resemblance: ☐ Mom   ☐ Dad

I hope the baby gets mom's:

_____

I hope the baby gets dad's:

_____

Advice for the Parents

_____
_____
_____
_____

Well Wishes for the Baby

_____
_____
_____
_____
_____

Guest Name

_____

Baby Predictions

Date of Birth: _____

Time of Birth: _____

Weight: _____   Height: _____

Hair Color: _____

Eye Color: _____

Resemblance: ☐ Mom   ☐ Dad

I hope the baby gets mom's:

_____

I hope the baby gets dad's:

_____

Advice for the Parents

_____
_____
_____
_____
_____

Well Wishes for the Baby

_____
_____
_____
_____
_____

Guest Name

_____

Baby Predictions

Date of Birth: _____

Time of Birth: _____

Weight: _____   Height: _____

Hair Color: _____

Eye Color: _____

Resemblance: ☐ Mom   ☐ Dad

I hope the baby gets mom's:

_____

I hope the baby gets dad's:

_____

Advice for the Parents

_____

_____

_____

_____

Well Wishes for the Baby

_____

_____

_____

_____

Guest Name

_____

Baby Predictions

Date of Birth: _____
Time of Birth: _____
Weight: _____   Height: _____
Hair Color: _____
Eye Color: _____
Resemblance: ☐ Mom   ☐ Dad

I hope the baby gets mom's:
_____

I hope the baby gets dad's:
_____

Advice for the Parents

_____
_____
_____
_____
_____

Well Wishes for the Baby

_____
_____
_____
_____
_____

Guest Name

_____

Baby Predictions

Date of Birth: _____
Time of Birth: _____
Weight: _____   Height: _____
Hair Color: _____
Eye Color: _____
Resemblance: ☐ Mom   ☐ Dad

I hope the baby gets mom's:
_____

I hope the baby gets dad's:
_____

Advice for the Parents

_____
_____
_____
_____
_____

Well Wishes for the Baby

_____
_____
_____
_____
_____

Guest Name

_____

Baby Predictions

Date of Birth: _____
Time of Birth: _____
Weight: _____   Height: _____
Hair Color: _____
Eye Color: _____
Resemblance: ☐ Mom   ☐ Dad

I hope the baby gets mom's:
_____

I hope the baby gets dad's:
_____

Advice for the Parents

_____
_____
_____
_____
_____

Well Wishes for the Baby

_____
_____
_____
_____
_____

Guest Name

_____

Baby Predictions

Date of Birth: _____
Time of Birth: _____
Weight: _____   Height: _____
Hair Color: _____
Eye Color: _____
Resemblance: ☐ Mom   ☐ Dad

I hope the baby gets mom's:
_____

I hope the baby gets dad's:
_____

Advice for the Parents

_____
_____
_____
_____
_____

Well Wishes for the Baby

_____
_____
_____
_____
_____

Guest Name

_____

Baby Predictions

Date of Birth: _____
Time of Birth: _____
Weight: _____   Height: _____
Hair Color: _____
Eye Color: _____
Resemblance: ☐ Mom   ☐ Dad

I hope the baby gets mom's:
_____

I hope the baby gets dad's:
_____

Advice for the Parents

_____
_____
_____
_____
_____

Well Wishes for the Baby

_____
_____
_____
_____
_____

Guest Name

_____

Baby Predictions

Date of Birth: _____
Time of Birth: _____
Weight: _____   Height: _____
Hair Color: _____
Eye Color: _____
Resemblance: ☐ Mom   ☐ Dad

I hope the baby gets mom's:
_____

I hope the baby gets dad's:
_____

Advice for the Parents

_____
_____
_____
_____
_____

Well Wishes for the Baby

_____
_____
_____
_____
_____

Guest Name

_____

Baby Predictions

Date of Birth: _____

Time of Birth: _____

Weight: _____   Height: _____

Hair Color: _____

Eye Color: _____

Resemblance: ☐ Mom   ☐ Dad

I hope the baby gets mom's:

_____

I hope the baby gets dad's:

_____

Advice for the Parents

_____
_____
_____
_____
_____

Well Wishes for the Baby

_____
_____
_____
_____

Guest Name

_____

Baby Predictions

Date of Birth: _____
Time of Birth: _____
Weight: _____   Height: _____
Hair Color: _____
Eye Color: _____
Resemblance: ☐ Mom   ☐ Dad

I hope the baby gets mom's:
_____

I hope the baby gets dad's:
_____

Advice for the Parents

_____
_____
_____
_____

Well Wishes for the Baby

_____
_____
_____
_____

Guest Name

_____

Baby Predictions

Date of Birth: _____

Time of Birth: _____

Weight: _____   Height: _____

Hair Color: _____

Eye Color: _____

Resemblance: ☐ Mom   ☐ Dad

I hope the baby gets mom's:

_____

I hope the baby gets dad's:

_____

Advice for the Parents

_____

_____

_____

_____

Well Wishes for the Baby

_____

_____

_____

_____

_____

Guest Name

_____

Baby Predictions

Date of Birth: _____
Time of Birth: _____
Weight: _____   Height: _____
Hair Color: _____
Eye Color: _____
Resemblance: ☐ Mom   ☐ Dad

I hope the baby gets mom's:
_____

I hope the baby gets dad's:
_____

Advice for the Parents

_____
_____
_____
_____

Well Wishes for the Baby

_____
_____
_____
_____
_____

Guest Name

_____

Baby Predictions

Date of Birth: _____
Time of Birth: _____
Weight: _____   Height: _____
Hair Color: _____
Eye Color: _____
Resemblance: ☐ Mom   ☐ Dad

I hope the baby gets mom's:
_____

I hope the baby gets dad's:
_____

Advice for the Parents

_____
_____
_____
_____
_____

Well Wishes for the Baby

_____
_____
_____
_____

Guest Name

_____

Baby Predictions

Date of Birth: _____

Time of Birth: _____

Weight: _____   Height: _____

Hair Color: _____

Eye Color: _____

Resemblance: ☐ Mom   ☐ Dad

I hope the baby gets mom's:

_____

I hope the baby gets dad's:

_____

Advice for the Parents

_____
_____
_____
_____
_____

Well Wishes for the Baby

_____
_____
_____
_____
_____

Guest Name

_____

Baby Predictions

Date of Birth: _____

Time of Birth: _____

Weight: _____   Height: _____

Hair Color: _____

Eye Color: _____

Resemblance: ☐ Mom   ☐ Dad

I hope the baby gets mom's:

_____

I hope the baby gets dad's:

_____

Advice for the Parents

_____
_____
_____
_____
_____

Well Wishes for the Baby

_____
_____
_____
_____
_____

Guest Name

_____

Baby Predictions

Date of Birth: _____
Time of Birth: _____
Weight: _____   Height: _____
Hair Color: _____
Eye Color: _____
Resemblance: ☐ Mom   ☐ Dad

I hope the baby gets mom's:
_____

I hope the baby gets dad's:
_____

Advice for the Parents

_____
_____
_____
_____

Well Wishes for the Baby

_____
_____
_____
_____
_____

Guest Name

_____

Baby Predictions

Date of Birth: _____

Time of Birth: _____

Weight: _____ Height: _____

Hair Color: _____

Eye Color: _____

Resemblance: ☐ Mom ☐ Dad

I hope the baby gets mom's:

_____

I hope the baby gets dad's:

_____

Advice for the Parents

_____

_____

_____

_____

Well Wishes for the Baby

_____

_____

_____

_____

_____

Guest Name

_____

Baby Predictions

Date of Birth: _____
Time of Birth: _____
Weight: _____   Height: _____
Hair Color: _____
Eye Color: _____
Resemblance: ☐ Mom   ☐ Dad

I hope the baby gets mom's:
_____

I hope the baby gets dad's:
_____

Advice for the Parents

_____
_____
_____
_____
_____

Well Wishes for the Baby

_____
_____
_____
_____
_____

Guest Name

_____

Baby Predictions

Date of Birth: _____

Time of Birth: _____

Weight: _____   Height: _____

Hair Color: _____

Eye Color: _____

Resemblance: ☐ Mom   ☐ Dad

I hope the baby gets mom's:

_____

I hope the baby gets dad's:

_____

Advice for the Parents

_____
_____
_____
_____
_____

Well Wishes for the Baby

_____
_____
_____
_____
_____

Guest Name

_____

Baby Predictions

Date of Birth: _____

Time of Birth: _____

Weight: _____   Height: _____

Hair Color: _____

Eye Color: _____

Resemblance: ☐ Mom   ☐ Dad

I hope the baby gets mom's:

_____

I hope the baby gets dad's:

_____

Advice for the Parents

_____

_____

_____

_____

_____

Well Wishes for the Baby

_____

_____

_____

_____

_____

Guest Name

_____

Baby Predictions

Date of Birth: _____
Time of Birth: _____
Weight: _____   Height: _____
Hair Color: _____
Eye Color: _____
Resemblance: ☐ Mom   ☐ Dad

I hope the baby gets mom's:
_____

I hope the baby gets dad's:
_____

Advice for the Parents

_____
_____
_____
_____

Well Wishes for the Baby

_____
_____
_____
_____
_____

Guest Name

_____

Baby Predictions

Date of Birth: _____
Time of Birth: _____
Weight: _____ Height: _____
Hair Color: _____
Eye Color: _____
Resemblance: ☐ Mom ☐ Dad

I hope the baby gets mom's:

_____

I hope the baby gets dad's:

_____

Advice for the Parents

_____
_____
_____
_____

Well Wishes for the Baby

_____
_____
_____
_____

Guest Name

_____

Baby Predictions

Date of Birth: _____

Time of Birth: _____

Weight: _____   Height: _____

Hair Color: _____

Eye Color: _____

Resemblance: ☐ Mom   ☐ Dad

I hope the baby gets mom's:

_____

I hope the baby gets dad's:

_____

Advice for the Parents

_____

_____

_____

_____

Well Wishes for the Baby

_____

_____

_____

_____

_____

Guest Name

_____

Baby Predictions

Date of Birth: _____

Time of Birth: _____

Weight: _____ Height: _____

Hair Color: _____

Eye Color: _____

Resemblance: ☐ Mom ☐ Dad

I hope the baby gets mom's:

_____

I hope the baby gets dad's:

_____

Advice for the Parents

_____
_____
_____
_____
_____

Well Wishes for the Baby

_____
_____
_____
_____
_____

Guest Name

_____

Baby Predictions

Date of Birth: _____
Time of Birth: _____
Weight: _____   Height: _____
Hair Color: _____
Eye Color: _____
Resemblance: ☐ Mom   ☐ Dad

I hope the baby gets mom's:
_____

I hope the baby gets dad's:
_____

Advice for the Parents

_____
_____
_____
_____

Well Wishes for the Baby

_____
_____
_____
_____

Guest Name

_____

Baby Predictions

Date of Birth: _____

Time of Birth: _____

Weight: _____   Height: _____

Hair Color: _____

Eye Color: _____

Resemblance: ☐ Mom   ☐ Dad

I hope the baby gets mom's:

_____

I hope the baby gets dad's:

_____

Advice for the Parents

_____

_____

_____

_____

_____

Well Wishes for the Baby

_____

_____

_____

_____

_____

Guest Name

_____

Baby Predictions

Date of Birth: _____

Time of Birth: _____

Weight: _____   Height: _____

Hair Color: _____

Eye Color: _____

Resemblance: ☐ Mom   ☐ Dad

I hope the baby gets mom's:

_____

I hope the baby gets dad's:

_____

Advice for the Parents

_____
_____
_____
_____
_____

Well Wishes for the Baby

_____
_____
_____
_____
_____

Guest Name

_____

Baby Predictions

Date of Birth: _____
Time of Birth: _____
Weight: _____   Height: _____
Hair Color: _____
Eye Color: _____
Resemblance: ☐ Mom   ☐ Dad

I hope the baby gets mom's:
_____

I hope the baby gets dad's:
_____

Advice for the Parents

_____
_____
_____
_____

Well Wishes for the Baby

_____
_____
_____
_____
_____

Guest Name

_____

Baby Predictions

Date of Birth: _____

Time of Birth: _____

Weight: _____   Height: _____

Hair Color: _____

Eye Color: _____

Resemblance: ☐ Mom   ☐ Dad

I hope the baby gets mom's:

_____

I hope the baby gets dad's:

_____

Advice for the Parents

_____
_____
_____
_____
_____

Well Wishes for the Baby

_____
_____
_____
_____
_____

Guest Name

_____

Baby Predictions

Date of Birth: _____

Time of Birth: _____

Weight: _____   Height: _____

Hair Color: _____

Eye Color: _____

Resemblance: ☐ Mom   ☐ Dad

I hope the baby gets mom's:

_____

I hope the baby gets dad's:

_____

Advice for the Parents

_____

_____

_____

_____

_____

Well Wishes for the Baby

_____

_____

_____

_____

_____

Guest Name

_____

Baby Predictions

Date of Birth: _____

Time of Birth: _____

Weight: _____   Height: _____

Hair Color: _____

Eye Color: _____

Resemblance: ☐ Mom   ☐ Dad

I hope the baby gets mom's:

_____

I hope the baby gets dad's:

_____

Advice for the Parents

_____

_____

_____

_____

Well Wishes for the Baby

_____

_____

_____

_____

Guest Name

_____

Baby Predictions

Date of Birth: _____

Time of Birth: _____

Weight: _____ Height: _____

Hair Color: _____

Eye Color: _____

Resemblance: ☐ Mom   ☐ Dad

I hope the baby gets mom's:

_____

I hope the baby gets dad's:

_____

Advice for the Parents

_____

_____

_____

_____

_____

Well Wishes for the Baby

_____

_____

_____

_____

_____

Guest Name

_____

Baby Predictions

Date of Birth: _____

Time of Birth: _____

Weight: _____   Height: _____

Hair Color: _____

Eye Color: _____

Resemblance: ☐ Mom   ☐ Dad

I hope the baby gets mom's:

_____

I hope the baby gets dad's:

_____

Advice for the Parents

_____
_____
_____
_____
_____

Well Wishes for the Baby

_____
_____
_____
_____
_____

Guest Name

_____

Baby Predictions

Date of Birth: _____

Time of Birth: _____

Weight: _____   Height: _____

Hair Color: _____

Eye Color: _____

Resemblance: ☐ Mom   ☐ Dad

I hope the baby gets mom's:

_____

I hope the baby gets dad's:

_____

Advice for the Parents

_____
_____
_____
_____
_____

Well Wishes for the Baby

_____
_____
_____
_____
_____

Guest Name

_____

Baby Predictions

Date of Birth: _____
Time of Birth: _____
Weight: _____   Height: _____
Hair Color: _____
Eye Color: _____
Resemblance: ☐ Mom   ☐ Dad

I hope the baby gets mom's:
_____

I hope the baby gets dad's:
_____

Advice for the Parents

_____
_____
_____
_____
_____

Well Wishes for the Baby

_____
_____
_____
_____
_____

Guest Name

_____

Baby Predictions

Date of Birth: _____
Time of Birth: _____
Weight: _____   Height: _____
Hair Color: _____
Eye Color: _____
Resemblance: ☐ Mom   ☐ Dad

I hope the baby gets mom's:
_____

I hope the baby gets dad's:
_____

Advice for the Parents

_____
_____
_____
_____
_____

Well Wishes for the Baby

_____
_____
_____
_____
_____

Guest Name

_____

Baby Predictions

Date of Birth: _____

Time of Birth: _____

Weight: _____   Height: _____

Hair Color: _____

Eye Color: _____

Resemblance: ☐ Mom   ☐ Dad

I hope the baby gets mom's:

_____

I hope the baby gets dad's:

_____

Advice for the Parents

_____

_____

_____

_____

Well Wishes for the Baby

_____

_____

_____

_____

_____

Guest Name

_____

Baby Predictions

Date of Birth: _____
Time of Birth: _____
Weight: _____   Height: _____
Hair Color: _____
Eye Color: _____
Resemblance: ☐ Mom   ☐ Dad

I hope the baby gets mom's:
_____

I hope the baby gets dad's:
_____

Advice for the Parents

_____
_____
_____
_____
_____

Well Wishes for the Baby

_____
_____
_____
_____

Guest Name

_____

Baby Predictions

Date of Birth: _____
Time of Birth: _____
Weight: _____   Height: _____
Hair Color: _____
Eye Color: _____
Resemblance: ☐ Mom   ☐ Dad

I hope the baby gets mom's:
_____

I hope the baby gets dad's:
_____

Advice for the Parents

_____
_____
_____
_____
_____

Well Wishes for the Baby

_____
_____
_____
_____
_____

Guest Name

_____

Baby Predictions

Date of Birth: _____

Time of Birth: _____

Weight: _____   Height: _____

Hair Color: _____

Eye Color: _____

Resemblance: ☐ Mom   ☐ Dad

I hope the baby gets mom's:

_____

I hope the baby gets dad's:

_____

Advice for the Parents

_____

_____

_____

_____

Well Wishes for the Baby

_____

_____

_____

_____

_____

Guest Name

_____

Baby Predictions

Date of Birth: _____

Time of Birth: _____

Weight: _____   Height: _____

Hair Color: _____

Eye Color: _____

Resemblance: ☐ Mom   ☐ Dad

I hope the baby gets mom's:

_____

I hope the baby gets dad's:

_____

Advice for the Parents

_____

_____

_____

_____

Well Wishes for the Baby

_____

_____

_____

_____

_____

Guest Name

_____

Baby Predictions

Date of Birth: _____

Time of Birth: _____

Weight: _____ Height: _____

Hair Color: _____

Eye Color: _____

Resemblance: ☐ Mom ☐ Dad

I hope the baby gets mom's:

_____

I hope the baby gets dad's:

_____

Advice for the Parents

_____

_____

_____

_____

_____

Well Wishes for the Baby

_____

_____

_____

_____

Guest Name

_____

Baby Predictions

Date of Birth: _____
Time of Birth: _____
Weight: _____   Height: _____
Hair Color: _____
Eye Color: _____
Resemblance: ☐ Mom   ☐ Dad

I hope the baby gets mom's:
_____

I hope the baby gets dad's:
_____

Advice for the Parents

_____
_____
_____
_____

Well Wishes for the Baby

_____
_____
_____
_____

Guest Name

_____

Baby Predictions

Date of Birth: _____

Time of Birth: _____

Weight: _____   Height: _____

Hair Color: _____

Eye Color: _____

Resemblance: ☐ Mom   ☐ Dad

I hope the baby gets mom's:

_____

I hope the baby gets dad's:

_____

Advice for the Parents

_____

_____

_____

_____

_____

Well Wishes for the Baby

_____

_____

_____

_____

Guest Name

_____

Baby Predictions

Date of Birth: _____

Time of Birth: _____

Weight: _____   Height: _____

Hair Color: _____

Eye Color: _____

Resemblance: ☐ Mom   ☐ Dad

I hope the baby gets mom's:

_____

I hope the baby gets dad's:

_____

Advice for the Parents

_____
_____
_____
_____
_____

Well Wishes for the Baby

_____
_____
_____
_____
_____

Guest Name

_____

Baby Predictions

Date of Birth: _____

Time of Birth: _____

Weight: _____ Height: _____

Hair Color: _____

Eye Color: _____

Resemblance: ☐ Mom ☐ Dad

I hope the baby gets mom's:

_____

I hope the baby gets dad's:

_____

Advice for the Parents

_____
_____
_____
_____
_____

Well Wishes for the Baby

_____
_____
_____
_____

Guest Name

_____

Baby Predictions

Date of Birth: _____

Time of Birth: _____

Weight: _____   Height: _____

Hair Color: _____

Eye Color: _____

Resemblance: ☐ Mom   ☐ Dad

I hope the baby gets mom's:

_____

I hope the baby gets dad's:

_____

Advice for the Parents

_____

_____

_____

_____

Well Wishes for the Baby

_____

_____

_____

_____

_____

Guest Name

_____

Baby Predictions

Date of Birth: _____

Time of Birth: _____

Weight: _____ Height: _____

Hair Color: _____

Eye Color: _____

Resemblance: ☐ Mom ☐ Dad

I hope the baby gets mom's:

_____

I hope the baby gets dad's:

_____

Advice for the Parents

_____

_____

_____

_____

Well Wishes for the Baby

_____

_____

_____

_____

_____

Guest Name

_____

Baby Predictions

Date of Birth: _____
Time of Birth: _____
Weight: _____   Height: _____
Hair Color: _____
Eye Color: _____
Resemblance: ☐ Mom   ☐ Dad

I hope the baby gets mom's:
_____

I hope the baby gets dad's:
_____

Advice for the Parents

_____
_____
_____
_____

Well Wishes for the Baby

_____
_____
_____
_____

Guest Name

_____

Baby Predictions

Date of Birth: _____
Time of Birth: _____
Weight: _____   Height: _____
Hair Color: _____
Eye Color: _____
Resemblance: ☐ Mom   ☐ Dad

I hope the baby gets mom's:
_____

I hope the baby gets dad's:
_____

Advice for the Parents

_____
_____
_____
_____
_____

Well Wishes for the Baby

_____
_____
_____
_____
_____

Guest Name

_____

Baby Predictions

Date of Birth: _____

Time of Birth: _____

Weight: _____   Height: _____

Hair Color: _____

Eye Color: _____

Resemblance: ☐ Mom   ☐ Dad

I hope the baby gets mom's:

_____

I hope the baby gets dad's:

_____

Advice for the Parents

_____
_____
_____
_____
_____

Well Wishes for the Baby

_____
_____
_____
_____
_____

Guest Name

_____

Baby Predictions

Date of Birth: _____

Time of Birth: _____

Weight: _____   Height: _____

Hair Color: _____

Eye Color: _____

Resemblance: ☐ Mom   ☐ Dad

I hope the baby gets mom's:

_____

I hope the baby gets dad's:

_____

Advice for the Parents

_____

_____

_____

_____

_____

Well Wishes for the Baby

_____

_____

_____

_____

_____

Guest Name

_____

Baby Predictions

Date of Birth: _____

Time of Birth: _____

Weight: _____ Height: _____

Hair Color: _____

Eye Color: _____

Resemblance: ☐ Mom ☐ Dad

I hope the baby gets mom's:

_____

I hope the baby gets dad's:

_____

Advice for the Parents

_____
_____
_____
_____

Well Wishes for the Baby

_____
_____
_____
_____

Guest Name

_____

Baby Predictions

Date of Birth: _____
Time of Birth: _____
Weight: _____   Height: _____
Hair Color: _____
Eye Color: _____
Resemblance: ☐ Mom   ☐ Dad

I hope the baby gets mom's:
_____

I hope the baby gets dad's:
_____

Advice for the Parents

_____
_____
_____
_____
_____

Well Wishes for the Baby

_____
_____
_____
_____

Guest Name

_____

Baby Predictions

Date of Birth: _____
Time of Birth: _____
Weight: _____ Height: _____
Hair Color: _____
Eye Color: _____
Resemblance: ☐ Mom ☐ Dad

I hope the baby gets mom's:
_____

I hope the baby gets dad's:
_____

Advice for the Parents

_____
_____
_____
_____

Well Wishes for the Baby

_____
_____
_____
_____

Guest Name

_____

Baby Predictions

Date of Birth: _____
Time of Birth: _____
Weight: _____   Height: _____
Hair Color: _____
Eye Color: _____
Resemblance: ☐ Mom   ☐ Dad

I hope the baby gets mom's:
_____

I hope the baby gets dad's:
_____

Advice for the Parents

_____
_____
_____
_____
_____

Well Wishes for the Baby

_____
_____
_____
_____
_____

Guest Name

_____

Baby Predictions

Date of Birth: _____
Time of Birth: _____
Weight: _____   Height: _____
Hair Color: _____
Eye Color: _____
Resemblance: ☐ Mom   ☐ Dad

I hope the baby gets mom's:

_____

I hope the baby gets dad's:

_____

Advice for the Parents

_____
_____
_____
_____

Well Wishes for the Baby

_____
_____
_____
_____
_____

Guest Name

_____

Baby Predictions

Date of Birth: _____
Time of Birth: _____
Weight: _____   Height: _____
Hair Color: _____
Eye Color: _____
Resemblance: ☐ Mom   ☐ Dad

I hope the baby gets mom's:
_____

I hope the baby gets dad's:
_____

Advice for the Parents

_____
_____
_____
_____

Well Wishes for the Baby

_____
_____
_____
_____

Guest Name

_____

Baby Predictions

Date of Birth: _____

Time of Birth: _____

Weight: _____   Height: _____

Hair Color: _____

Eye Color: _____

Resemblance: ☐ Mom   ☐ Dad

I hope the baby gets mom's:

_____

I hope the baby gets dad's:

_____

Advice for the Parents

_____

_____

_____

_____

Well Wishes for the Baby

_____

_____

_____

_____

_____

Guest Name

_____

Baby Predictions

Date of Birth: _____
Time of Birth: _____
Weight: _____ Height: _____
Hair Color: _____
Eye Color: _____
Resemblance: ☐ Mom ☐ Dad

I hope the baby gets mom's:
_____

I hope the baby gets dad's:
_____

Advice for the Parents

_____
_____
_____
_____
_____

Well Wishes for the Baby

_____
_____
_____
_____
_____

Guest Name

_____

Baby Predictions

Date of Birth: _____
Time of Birth: _____
Weight: _____   Height: _____
Hair Color: _____
Eye Color: _____
Resemblance: ☐ Mom   ☐ Dad

I hope the baby gets mom's:
_____

I hope the baby gets dad's:
_____

Advice for the Parents

_____
_____
_____
_____
_____

Well Wishes for the Baby

_____
_____
_____
_____
_____

Guest Name

_____

Baby Predictions

Date of Birth: _____
Time of Birth: _____
Weight: _____ Height: _____
Hair Color: _____
Eye Color: _____
Resemblance: ☐ Mom ☐ Dad

I hope the baby gets mom's:
_____

I hope the baby gets dad's:
_____

Advice for the Parents

_____
_____
_____
_____
_____

Well Wishes for the Baby

_____
_____
_____
_____
_____

Guest Name

_____

Baby Predictions

Date of Birth: _____

Time of Birth: _____

Weight: _____   Height: _____

Hair Color: _____

Eye Color: _____

Resemblance: ☐ Mom   ☐ Dad

I hope the baby gets mom's:

_____

I hope the baby gets dad's:

_____

Advice for the Parents

_____

_____

_____

_____

Well Wishes for the Baby

_____

_____

_____

_____

_____

Guest Name

_____

Baby Predictions

Date of Birth: _____

Time of Birth: _____

Weight: _____ Height: _____

Hair Color: _____

Eye Color: _____

Resemblance: ☐ Mom ☐ Dad

I hope the baby gets mom's:

_____

I hope the baby gets dad's:

_____

Advice for the Parents

_____
_____
_____
_____
_____

Well Wishes for the Baby

_____
_____
_____
_____
_____

Guest Name

_____

Baby Predictions

Date of Birth: _____

Time of Birth: _____

Weight: _____   Height: _____

Hair Color: _____

Eye Color: _____

Resemblance: ☐ Mom   ☐ Dad

I hope the baby gets mom's:

_____

I hope the baby gets dad's:

_____

Advice for the Parents

_____

_____

_____

_____

_____

Well Wishes for the Baby

_____

_____

_____

_____

_____

Guest Name

_____

Baby Predictions

Date of Birth: _____

Time of Birth: _____

Weight: _____   Height: _____

Hair Color: _____

Eye Color: _____

Resemblance: ☐ Mom   ☐ Dad

I hope the baby gets mom's:

_____

I hope the baby gets dad's:

_____

Advice for the Parents

_____

_____

_____

_____

_____

Well Wishes for the Baby

_____

_____

_____

_____

_____

Guest Name

_____

Baby Predictions

Date of Birth: _____
Time of Birth: _____
Weight: _____   Height: _____
Hair Color: _____
Eye Color: _____
Resemblance: ☐ Mom   ☐ Dad

I hope the baby gets mom's:
_____

I hope the baby gets dad's:
_____

Advice for the Parents

_____
_____
_____
_____
_____

Well Wishes for the Baby

_____
_____
_____
_____
_____

Guest Name

_____

Baby Predictions

Date of Birth: _____

Time of Birth: _____

Weight: _____   Height: _____

Hair Color: _____

Eye Color: _____

Resemblance: ☐ Mom   ☐ Dad

I hope the baby gets mom's:

_____

I hope the baby gets dad's:

_____

Advice for the Parents

_____
_____
_____
_____
_____

Well Wishes for the Baby

_____
_____
_____
_____
_____

Gift Log

Name	Gift
_____	_____
_____	_____
_____	_____
_____	_____
_____	_____
_____	_____
_____	_____
_____	_____
_____	_____

Gift Log

Name	Gift
_____	_____
_____	_____
_____	_____
_____	_____
_____	_____
_____	_____
_____	_____
_____	_____
_____	_____
_____	_____

Gift Log

Name   Gift

_____   _____

_____   _____

_____   _____

_____   _____

_____   _____

_____   _____

_____   _____

_____   _____

_____   _____

_____   _____

Gift Log

Name	Gift
_____	_____
_____	_____
_____	_____
_____	_____
_____	_____
_____	_____
_____	_____
_____	_____
_____	_____

Gift Log

Name	Gift
_____	_____
_____	_____
_____	_____
_____	_____
_____	_____
_____	_____
_____	_____
_____	_____
_____	_____